VEGETABLES/VEGETALES

by/por Tea Benduhn

Reading consultant/Consultora de lectura: Susan Nations, M.Ed.,
author, literacy coach, consultant in literacy development/
autora, tutora de alfabetización, consultora de desarrollo de la lectura

WEEKLY READER®
PUBLISHING

Please visit our web site at: www.garethstevens.com
For a free color catalog describing our list of high-quality books,
call 1-800-542-2595 (USA) or 1-800-387-3178 (Canada).

Library of Congress Cataloging-in-Publication Data available upon request from publisher.

ISBN: 978-0-8368-8459-3 (lib. bdg.)
ISBN: 978-0-8368-8466-1 (softcover)

This edition first published in 2008 by
Weekly Reader® Books
An imprint of Gareth Stevens Publishing
1 Reader's Digest Road
Pleasantville, NY 10570-7000 USA

Managing editor: Valerie J. Weber
Art direction: Tammy West
Graphic designer: Scott Krall
Picture research: Diane Laska-Swanke
Photographer: Gregg Andersen
Production: Jessica Yanke
Spanish translation: Tatiana Acosta and Guillermo Gutiérrez

Printed in the United States of America

1 2 3 4 5 6 7 8 9 11 10 09 08 07

Note to Educators and Parents

Reading is such an exciting adventure for young children! They are beginning to integrate their oral language skills with written language. To encourage children along the path to early literacy, books must be colorful, engaging, and interesting; they should invite the young reader to explore both the print and the pictures.

The *Find Out About Food* series is designed to help children understand the value of good nutrition and eating to stay healthy. In each book, young readers will learn how their favorite foods — and possibly some new ones — fit into a balanced diet.

Each book is specially designed to support the young reader in the reading process. The familiar topics are appealing to young children and invite them to read — and re-read — again and again. The full-color photographs and enhanced text further support the student during the reading process.

In addition to serving as wonderful picture books in schools, libraries, homes, and other places where children learn to love reading, these books are specifically intended to be read within an instructional guided reading group. This small group setting allows beginning readers to work with a fluent adult model as they make meaning from the text. After children develop fluency with the text and content, the book can be read independently. Children and adults alike will find these books supportive, engaging, and fun!

— Susan Nations, M.Ed., author, literacy coach, and consultant in literacy development

Nota para los maestros y los padres

¡Leer es una aventura tan emocionante para los niños pequeños! A esta edad están comenzando a integrar su manejo del lenguaje oral con el lenguaje escrito. Para animar a los niños en el camino de la lectura incipiente, los libros deben ser coloridos, estimulantes e interesantes; deben invitar a los jóvenes lectores a explorar la letra impresa y las ilustraciones.

Conoce la comida es una colección diseñada para ayudar a los jóvenes lectores a entender la importancia de una nutrición apropiada y el papel de la alimentación en la salud. En cada libro, los jóvenes lectores aprenderán de qué forma sus alimentos favoritos —y posiblemente algunos nuevos— pueden formar parte de una dieta balanceada.

Cada libro está especialmente diseñado para ayudar a los jóvenes lectores en el proceso de lectura. Los temas familiares llaman la atención de los niños y los invitan a leer una y otra vez. Las fotografías a todo color y el tamaño de la letra ayudan aún más al estudiante en el proceso de lectura.

Además de servir como maravillosos libros ilustrados en escuelas, bibliotecas, hogares y otros lugares donde los niños aprenden a amar la lectura, estos libros han sido especialmente concebidos para ser leídos en un grupo de lectura guiada. Este contexto permite que los lectores incipientes trabajen con un adulto que domina la lectura mientras van determinando el significado del texto. Una vez que los niños dominan el texto y el contenido, el libro puede ser leído de manera independiente. ¡Estos libros les resultarán útiles, estimulantes y divertidos a niños y a adultos por igual!

— Susan Nations, M.Ed., autora, tutora de alfabetización, consultora de desarrollo de la lectura

Dad tells me to eat my vegetables.
Why should I?

Papá insiste en que me coma
los vegetales. ¿Por qué tendría
que hacerlo?

Vegetables are part of the **food pyramid**. The six colored bands on the food pyramid stand for types of foods. Make smart choices. Eat these foods and **exercise** every day.

Los vegetales son parte de la **pirámide alimentaria**. Cada una de las seis franjas de colores de la pirámide representa un tipo de alimento. Elige de forma inteligente. Consume estos alimentos y haz **ejercicio** todos los días.

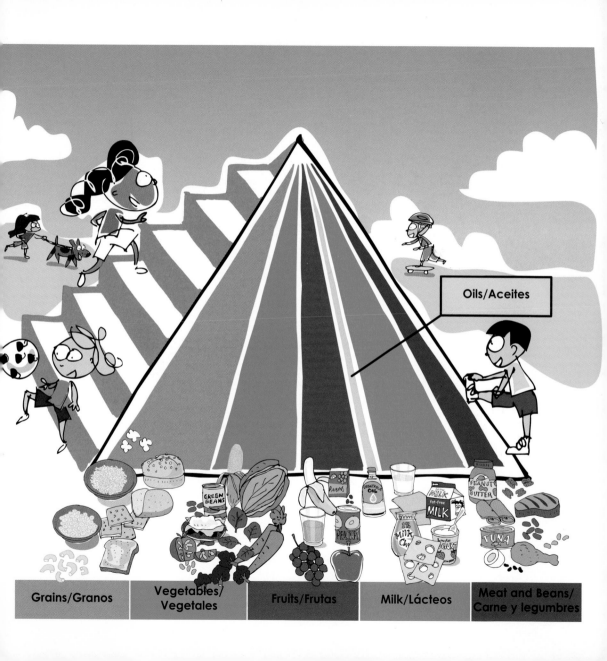

Oils/Aceites

Grains/Granos

Vegetables/
Vegetales

Fruits/Frutas

Milk/Lácteos

Meat and Beans/
Carne y legumbres

The wide green band stands for vegetables. The width means that you should eat lots of vegetables.

La franja verde ancha representa los vegetales. El grosor de la banda indica que debes comer muchos vegetales.

There are lots of kinds of vegetables. Some vegetables taste good raw. Peppers, tomatoes, and cucumbers are good in a salad.

Hay vegetales de muchos tipos. Algunos están ricos crudos. Pimientos, tomates y pepinos se pueden comer en una sabrosa ensalada.

Green beans and broccoli are dark green vegetables. They taste good raw or cooked. I like to eat steamed broccoli.

Los ejotes y el brócoli son de color verde oscuro. Están ricos crudos o cocidos. A mí me gusta comer brócoli al vapor.

Carrots and sweet potatoes are orange vegetables. Carrots can be made into juice. Carrot juice tastes sweet.

Las zanahorias y el camote son de color naranja. Con las zanahorias se puede hacer jugo. El jugo de zanahoria es dulce.

Vegetables make your teeth and gums **healthy**. They make your eyes and skin healthy, too. Eating vegetables helps heal cuts and wounds.

Comer vegetales te ayuda a tener dientes y encías **saludables**. También contribuye a la salud de tus ojos y de tu piel. Comer vegetales hace que sanen más rápido las cortaduras y las heridas.

17

Vegetables can also make your meals fun! Crisp vegetables make crunchy sounds.

¡Los vegetales también pueden hacer que las comidas sean más divertidas! Los vegetales frescos crujen cuando los masticas.

19

How can you eat enough vegetables? Eat them for your main meal! Vegetable stir-fry, vegetable soup, and vegetable pizza taste good. What kind of vegetable will you try next?

¿Qué puedes hacer para comer suficientes vegetales? ¡Haz que sean tu principal comida! Los vegetales salteados, la sopa de vegetales y la *pizza* con vegetales están todos muy ricos. ¿Qué nuevo vegetal vas a probar?

Glossary/Glosario

food pyramid — the drawing that shows six colored bands that stand for the six different food groups people should eat every day

heal — to become well again and free from injury

healthy — strong and free from illness

raw — uncooked

steamed — cooked by steam

----

al vapor — cocido con vapor

crudo — sin cocinar

pirámide alimentaria — dibujo que muestra seis franjas de colores que representan seis grupos diferentes de alimentos que las personas deben comer a diario

saludable — fuerte y sin enfermedades

sanar — recuperar la salud y mejorarse de lesiones

For More Information/Más información

Books/Libros

Fruits and Vegetables/Frutas y vegetales.
English and Spanish Foundations Series.
Gladys Rosa-Mendoza (me+me publishing)

Las verduras. Los grupos de alimentos (series).
Robin Nelson (Lerner Publications)

The Vegetables Group. Pebble Plus (series).
Mari C. Schuh (Capstone)

Web Sites/Páginas Web

My Pyramid for Kids

mypyramid.gov/kids/index.html
Click on links to play a game and learn more at the
government's Web site about the food pyramid.

Publisher's note to educators and parents: Our editors have carefully reviewed this
Web site to ensure that it is suitable for children. Many Web sites change frequently,
however, and we cannot guarantee that a site's future contents will continue to
meet our high standards of quality and educational value. Be advised that children
should be closely supervised whenever they access the Internet.

Index/Índice

About the Author/Información sobre la autora

Tea Benduhn writes and edits books for children and teens. She lives in the beautiful state of Wisconsin with her husband and two cats. The walls of their home are lined with bookshelves filled with books. Tea says, "I read every day. It is more fun than watching television!"

Tea Benduhn escribe y corrige libros para niños y adolescentes. Vive en el bello estado de Wisconsin con su esposo y dos gatos. Las paredes de su casa están cubiertas de estanterías con libros. Tea dice: "Leo todos los días. ¡Es más divertido que ver televisión!".